10.95

D0759244

DATE DUE		
DEC 1 8		
NOV. 1 7		
MAR 2 7		
DEC 8		

Discard

$10.95
959.704   Edwards, Richard
Edw   The Vietnam war
Copy 1

111795

Golden Sierra
High School Library

THE VIETNAM WAR

Richard Edwards

ROURKE ENTERPRISES, INC.
Vero Beach, Florida 32964

111795

Golden Sierra
High School Library

First published in the United States in 1986 by
Rourke Enterprises, Inc.
Vero Beach, Florida 32964

First published in 1986 by
Wayland (Publishers) Ltd
61 Western Road, Hove
East Sussex BN3 1JD, England

© Copyright 1986 Wayland (Publishers) Ltd

Typeset, printed and bound in Great Britain at
The Bath Press, Avon

Library of Congress Cataloging-in-Publication Data
Edwards, Richard, 1943 –
  The Vietnam war.
  (Flashpoints)
  Bibliography: p.
  Includes index.
  Summary: Discusses the origins, events, conclusion, and
aftermath of the conflict in Vietnam, as well as the
reactions and attitudes of the American public.
  1. Vietnamese Conflict, 1961–1975 – Juvenile
literature. [I. Vietnamese Conflict, 1961–1975]
I. Title   II. Series: Flashpoints.

DS557.7.E39   1987   956.704′3   86–20295

ISBN 0–86592–031–1

Contents

1 The spark to the tinder 8
2 The nationalist heritage 12
3 The Cold War 17
4 The civil war 22
5 The overthrow of Diem 27
6 Into the mire 31
7 The Tet Offensive 37
8 The antiwar movement 44
9 Nixon's war 51
10 Peace, war, reunification 57
11 America, post-Vietnam 63
12 Vietnam: the aftermath 68
Glossary 74
Index 76

1
The spark to the tinder

On August 2, 1964, the destroyer, USS *Maddox*, sailed into the Gulf of Tonkin off North Vietnam. Its task was to monitor electronically the effectiveness of South Vietnamese raids against Northern ports and radar installations. The *Maddox* sailed to within eight miles of the coast, well outside the international territorial limit of three miles. However, the North Vietnamese had declared a limit of twelve miles. They sent patrol boats to pursue and attempt to sink the *Maddox*. Two patrol boats were sunk and the *Maddox* returned to deeper waters.

The destroyer USS Turner Joy on patrol in the Gulf of Tonkin.

Two days later, on a similar mission, the *Maddox*, supported by another destroyer, the USS *Turner Joy*, returned to the same area and the two ships were involved in an "engagement." In a raging tropical storm, with electronic instruments going haywire, the captains presumed that they had come under attack. Both ships proceeded to fire at the unseen enemy. In fact, no attack had taken place. However, this second "incident" was taken by the American military commanders as justification for retaliatory action against North Vietnam, which they had long recommended.

Late on August 4, 1964, the United States began its first

The first American marines landing at Da Nang in March 1965.

9

A memorial to some of the thousands of American troops killed in the Vietnam War.

bombing raid against North Vietnam, adding a new dimension to the slowly escalating conflict between the South Vietnamese government and the Vietcong (South Vietnamese Communists). It was from this point that the possibilities of direct American involvement were to increase radically. In the eight and a half years to the signing of the Paris Peace Accord in 1973, this resulted in the dropping of a greater tonnage of bombs on Vietnam than the Allies had dropped during the whole of World War II.

On March 8, 1965, having despaired that the South Vietnamese Army could defeat the Vietcong on their own, the first American marines splashed ashore at Da Nang. By the end of the year there were 200,000 American troops in Vietnam, a figure which at its height in 1967 was to reach 540,000. Thus, what has become known as the tragedy of Vietnam unfolded; its eventual economic cost incalculable; the human losses immense. Exact figures are unavailable. It is estimated that between 1965 and 1973, the United States spent 120 *billion* dollars in Vietnam. The loss of life among North Vietnamese as a result of American bombing

is put at 1.5 million. About 924,000 Vietcong and North Vietnamese were killed in the South. However, this figure is unreliable, as many ordinary villagers were classified as Vietcong to improve the "body-count," which was supposed to show Americans at home that the war was being won. South Vietnamese losses are put at 183,000, while 58,000 American troops died fighting in a country no bigger than the state of Florida.

These figures tell their own story. One of the central questions to stem from them is why and how, despite these huge losses, it was the Vietcong and North Vietnamese who were eventually victorious. The United States, the leading military power in the world, took on an initially poorly equipped guerrilla army and lost; the inconceivable was realized. Greater firepower proved insufficient. The United States never really accepted this and it was that failure, combined with a lack of understanding of the nature of the Vietnamese people, that resulted in a phantom encounter involving two American destroyers developing into what was to become an increasingly tragic war.

2
The nationalist heritage

An Annamite village submits to French troops in 1861. Annam was a region of French Indo-China. (See map opposite.)

The Vietnamese have a long tradition of opposition to foreign intervention in their country. For two thousand years before the French established colonial rule in 1887, the Vietnamese had defended their northern border against the Chinese – on many occasions unsuccessfully. Eventually, it was the payment of an annual tribute to the Chinese emperor that put an end to Chinese intervention. However, distrust of their neighbor's intentions continued, as it still does.

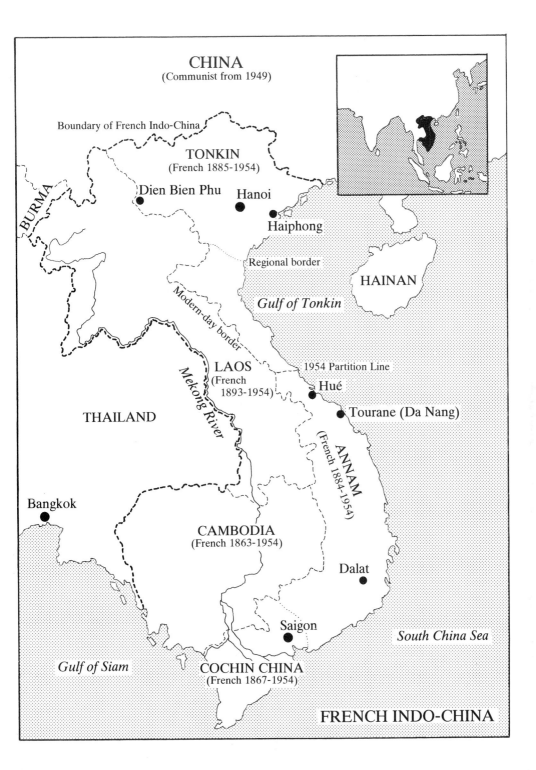

CHINA
(Communist from 1949)

Boundary of French Indo-China

TONKIN
(French 1885-1954)

Dien Bien Phu   Hanoi

Haiphong

BURMA

Regional border

HAINAN

Gulf of Tonkin

Modern-day border

LAOS
(French
1893-1954)

1954 Partition Line

Hué

Tourane (Da Nang)

THAILAND

Mekong River

ANNAM
(French 1884-1954)

Bangkok

CAMBODIA
(French 1863-1954)

Dalat

Saigon

South China Sea

Gulf of Siam

COCHIN CHINA
(French 1867-1954)

FRENCH INDO-CHINA

French Indo-China

In the nineteenth century, the industrialized nations of Europe were vying with each other for control of the resources and markets of the world. French intervention in Vietnam began in 1843, when a permanent fleet was deployed in Asian waters to protect France's trading privileges. These had been secured by the Jesuit priests who had been active in Vietnam for two centuries. Converting the Confucian and Buddhist mandarins and people to Christianity was only one aspect of their mission. It was the plans to eliminate Christianity of the Emperor Tu Duc who ascended the throne in 1847, which led to military intervention by the French and the establishment in 1887 of French Indo-China, incorporating Vietnam, Cambodia (now Kampuchea), and Laos.

From then until the outbreak of World War II in 1939, the French attempted to "civilize" the Vietnamese into the ways of French culture and ideas, to alter their way of life. Many of the Vietnamese leaders, on both sides, who were to be prominent in the Vietnam war twenty-five years later, including Ho Chi Minh, were educated by the French. However, while there was opposition to French rule and attempts to gain reforms, Vietnamese nationalists were ill-organized and lacked a clear idea of the course they should take. World War II, and the return of Ho Chi Minh after thirty years in exile, were to change that situation dramatically.

Formation of the Vietminh

Ho Chi Minh left Vietnam in 1911 at the age of twenty-one, a nationalist opposed to French rule, who hoped that by appealing to the revolutionary tradition of France, he would persuade her to return his homeland's independence. This hope proved ill-founded. In the wake of the Russian Revolution of 1917 and on reading Lenin's theory that national liberation could only be achieved through social revolution, Ho became a Communist. In 1924, he moved to Moscow, from where he traveled widely as an agent. In 1930, he was a cofounder of the Indo-China Communist Party. Its task was to organize and agitate against French rule. When Ho returned to Vietnam in 1941, although small in numbers, the Communist Party was the best organized of the opposition groups and was untainted by any previous cooperation with the French colonial authorities. The time had come for armed opposition to the foreigners.

Vietnam was under French rule until 1945. Although the Japanese had invaded Indo-China in 1940, the French government, now in alliance with Hitler in Europe, was left in power. In 1941, Ho formed the Vietminh (a broad nationalist group in which Communists took the leading role) to fight a guerrilla war against the French and Japanese. Although wary of Ho's Communist background, the Americans provided covert supplies and training for the Vietminh. Frustrated by the French government's inability to quell the Vietminh, the Japanese took direct control of running the country of March 9, 1945, five months before their capitulation to the Americans.

Ho Chi Minh reading a report during his guerrilla war against the French in the early 1940s.

Ho Chi Minh declaring Vietnam to be an independent state on September 2, 1945.

The Vietminh's objective was to defeat the Japanese, without the reestablishment of French rule. After the Japanese surrender in August 1945, Ho proclaimed a provisional Vietnamese government in Hanoi. On September 2, basing his speech on the American Declaration of Independence, Ho, with the support of leaders throughout Vietnam, declared the country an independent state. However, recognition, particularly from the US, which Ho saw as crucial, was not forthcoming. The French themselves were openly hostile to Vietnamese independence, and the growing tension between the Vietminh and French was to result eventually in the bombardment of Haiphong by French warships in November 1946. In retaliation, the Vietminh attacked French garrisons and retreated to the countryside to take up the war against the French. The independence of Vietnam had not been recognized and the war to establish the right to self-rule was firmly under way.

3
The Cold War

With the end of World War II came the breakup of the temporary alliance between the West and the USSR. Distrust of each other's intentions soon replaced the military priority of defeating the Axis powers (Germany, Italy, and Japan). Each side saw the other as a threat to its stability and way of life, and proceeded to build defense and propaganda machines against the other. However, direct conflict between the United States and the USSR, although contemplated, was thought to be untenable. The stage, therefore, moved to the growing anticolonial movements in the Third

Emperor Bao Dai. The French tried to reestablish his authority in 1949, but they were unsuccessful.

French soldiers in their trench at Dien Bien Phu.

World. The USSR was idealogically committed to the support of national liberation movements. The United States supported movements seeking independence from foreign rule, but was hostile to possible Communist influence in these movements. It saw itself as defending the "free world" against the totalitarianism of communism. The US, therefore, developed a policy of "containment," whereby Communist countries in existence at the end of World War II would not be directly threatened, but the United States would use its economic and military might to ensure that communism did not spread.

With Mao Zedong's victory in China in 1949 and the outbreak of the Korean War in 1950, the American focus of attention shifted to Asia and the containment of Chinese communism. It was felt that if Vietnam was allowed to

fall to the Vietminh, the rest of Southeast Asia would become Communist, country by country. That was the famous "Domino Theory," by which the United States justified its support for the French after World War II. But the Domino Theory tended to ignore two facts. First, that Vietnam was the only country in Southeast Asia where the Communists were well organized and popular. Second, the independence Ho tried to maintain from both Soviet and Chinese influence.

By 1950, the Vietminh were operating throughout Vietnam, harassing and killing French troops and officials. Militarily, the Vietminh fought a guerrilla war, taking control of the countryside, while leaving towns and cities in the hands of the French authorities. In the areas under their control, the Vietminh organized the peasants, introduced land reforms, established village councils and introduced literacy classes. These measures gained a good deal of support for the Vietminh and bound the peasants to their fight against the French. On January 14, 1950, Ho declared Vietnam a democratic republic and was instantly recognized as the legitimate government by the USSR and China.

Once again Ho hoped for support from the United States. However, the growing Cold War mentality of the US with its hostility to any person or movement associated with communism, was leading it in a different direction. The global issue of capitalism versus communism outweighed the local

Thousands of French officers and soldiers at Dien Bien Phu leaving their trenches and surrendering to the Vietnam People's Army.

Golden Sierra High School Library

issues in Vietnam. The French had never been able to reestablish complete colonial control over Indo-China after World War II and sought to reach agreements with certain nationalist leaders, whereby independence would be granted to their countries within limits. In Vietnam, they attempted to reestablish the authority of the Emperor Bao Dai, who returned from exile in 1949. However, this proved unsuccessful, as his reliance on the French undermined his credibility as a nationalist leader. In an attempt to gain the upper hand, the French called upon the United States for aid to fight the Vietminh. While unprepared to commit troops, as they were doing in Korea, the US provided millions of dollars in economic and military aid. By 1954, the United States was paying for eighty percent of the French war. However, the French were suffering mounting defeats and casualties.

Partition of Vietnam

On March 13, 1954, the battle of Dien Bien Phu began. That was to prove decisive. The previous January, the foreign ministers of the United States, Britain, France, and the USSR had met and agreed to a conference on Korea and Indo-China. The defeat of the French at Dien Bien

The ceasefire agreement being signed in Geneva after the defeat of the French at the Battle of Dien Bien Phu in May 1954.

Effigies of General de Gaulle and Ho Chi Minh hang hand in hand to commemorate July 20, 1954, "National Shame Day," when the Geneva Accord was signed, partitioning Vietnam.

Phu on May 7 spelled the end of colonial rule. The problem was what was to happen next? The Western powers were prepared for Vietnam to be independent, but did not want Communist control of the country. In July, at a conference in Geneva, a ceasefire was agreed. This was to be followed by the temporary partition of Vietnam at the seventeenth parallel, with each side withdrawing its troops and supporters: Vietminh to the North; French and non-Vietminh to the South. This was to be followed in 1956 by elections for the government of a reunified Vietnam. It was accepted on all sides that these elections would bring Ho to power. It was the failure to hold them that removed the solution of Vietnam's independence from the political arena back to the military one.

21

4
The civil war

The 1954 Geneva Accord was denounced by Bao Dai's government as a sellout to the Vietminh. Head of the government was Ngo Dinh Diem, a Catholic from central Vietnam, who, after the partition, began to build his support on the large number of Catholics who had emigrated to the South. These people feared the consequences of the proposed elections and looked to the United States for aid. This was forthcoming. Although the US had not dissented from the Geneva Accord, neither had she agreed to its implementation. On July 16, 1955, Diem discarded the Geneva Accord and the nationwide elections. This decision was supported by the United States, who had already begun to supply aid to Diem's government and agreed to train the South Vietnamese Army. How much Diem's decision was prompted by American support and a knowledge of the policy of containment is open to debate.

Civil war starts

With American backing, Diem declared the South as the Republic of Vietnam, with himself as president, thereby attempting to make permanent the temporary division of the country. He then began to return land which had been redistributed by the Vietminh to the original landlords and used the army to put down any opposition. Many thousands were jailed. Former members of the Vietminh, who had stayed in the South to prepare for the election, began to return to guerrilla activities. In October 1957, they began a coordinated campaign of assassination of government officials. That began the civil war that was to bring increasing chaos to the South, until the American military intervention in 1965.

The North was initially reluctant to be drawn into fighting the Diem government. It believed that the major powers would force Diem to honor the Geneva Accord. However,

Opposite *President Diem (center) walks down the steps of the Capitol in Washington with Vice-President Nixon after addressing Congress.*

Saigon 1962: twelve Communist students listen to the verdict of a military tribunal after being accused of conspiring to kill the American Ambassador. Four of them were sentenced to death, the remainder to prison.

the Western powers were reluctant to oppose American policy, being financially dependent on the United States for their postwar recovery. The North Vietnamese could not even depend on the support of the Communist countries. In January 1957, the USSR proposed that the United Nations recognize both the North and South Vietnamese governments, a move designed to improve its relations with the US. The Chinese were also prepared to see Vietnam divided, but that was in order to increase her influence on the North. The latter was dependent on food aid from the Chinese, as the partition had cut the North off from the main food-producing area of the Mekong River's delta. North Vietnam found herself unsupported diplomatically in her call for nationwide elections.

Further, she had problems of her own. In 1955, the Vietminh government had called for a rural revolution, the denouncement of rich peasants and landlords. This policy led to food production being reduced to a trickle, as peasants sought to settle personal scores by exposing rivals as enemies. Famine, starvation, and revolts resulted from this policy and it was only after it had been abandoned that relative peace was restored to the North.

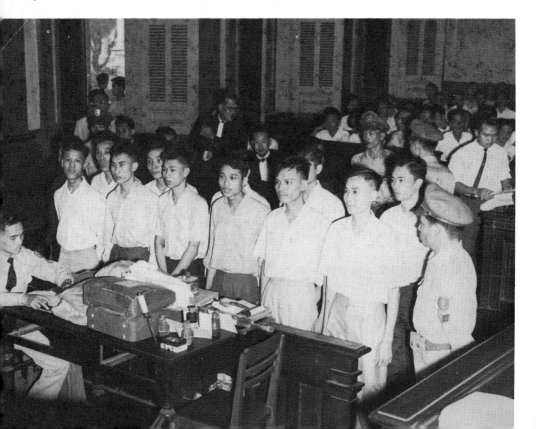

Thus it was only in 1959 that the North began to send aid to the Vietcong in the South. As Diem attempted to impose his authority on the Southern population, so opposition to him grew. As a consequence, American aid increased to improve the effectiveness of Diem's government and the army. A broad spectrum of opinion opposed Diem. However, as with the Vietminh, it was the Communists who were the best organized, militarily and politically, among the opposition and, as such, began to attract a lot of non-Communist support to them. As the aid began to flow from the North down the Ho Chi Minh Trail through Laos and Cambodia (Kampuchea), the predominance of the Communists in the opposition increased. This Trail (initially a series of paths through the tropical forests, but later to become a major roadway despite continuous American bombing)

Ho Chi Minh meeting Mao Zedong in China.

was essential to the Vietcong's war effort. Arms, medical supplies, Southern cadres (nonregular fighters) who had gone North in 1954, and eventually North Vietnamese troops, were to make the long trek from the North to the South.

Diem's government and army could do little to stem this flow, or the support given to the Vietcong by the Southern peasants, despite the continuous stream of American aid and personnel. Victory was continually proclaimed to be close at hand by Diem and the American officials in the South, but the longer the civil war went on, the more the internal opposition grew.

Aid to Communist forces in South Vietnam came from the North via the Ho Chi Minh Trail, and also from Cambodia (Kampuchea) via the Sihanouk Trail.

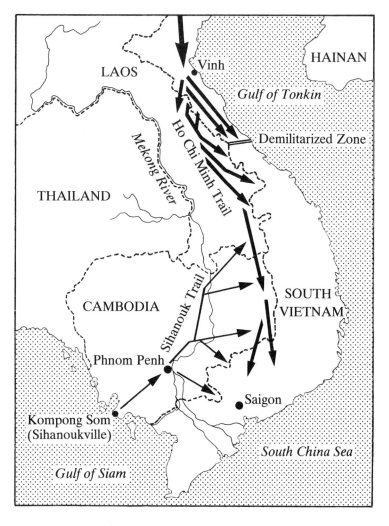

5
The overthrow of Diem

By 1963, the Diem government was receiving about $1 billion annually from the US and had 15,000 American military advisers. However, Diem's popularity continued to decline and he was not winning the civil war. His was a corrupt and brutal regime. Thousands of political opponents died in jail, Communist and non-Communist alike. Large amounts of American aid simply disappeared. The money intended to improve the standard of living of the peasants and ordinary soldiers never found its way to them. Military commanders and government officials manipulated the aid programs for their own benefit. Diem's troops, seeing their officers enriching themselves, lacked the morale to fight the Vietcong effectively. They took to looting villages, killing and raping their inhabitants. Inevitably, rural support for the Saigon government declined. Diem became reliant on city-based support, but as discontent grew there, he concentrated power in his own hands and those of his immediate family, distrusting the support of others. American officials started to see Diem as a puppet pulling his own strings, always wanting more aid, but never using it effectively.

Discontent increases
The 1962 Strategic Hamlets Program is typical of many of the policies adopted in the South to try to gain support for Diem. The United States proposed a two-pronged approach to the civil war. One prong was military. The second was the policy of "pacification": through reforms and by pumping aid into the villages, it was intended to build peasant support for the government and to isolate the Vietcong from their rural power base. The Strategic Hamlets Program was the attempt to move peasants into specially built villages, away from possible contact with the Vietcong. This Program proved to be a total failure and only served to distance the peasantry from Diem's govern-

Civilians try to storm the presidential palace in Saigon during the coup which resulted in President Diem's overthrow.

ment. Vietnam is essentially a rural country. The peasants' home and land is integral to the ancestor worship that is part of traditional Vietnamese culture. In forcibly moving the peasants to new homes, Diem's government was, in effect, tearing them away from their ancestors. The peasants did not want to move and, as soon as they could, returned to their own villages. The whole of the Strategic Hamlets Program disintegrated.

This is one of many examples of where a course of action, conceived to undermine support for the Vietcong, may actually have increased it. The Vietcong were more sensitive to the traditional pattern of Vietnamese life.

It was not only the peasants and Vietcong who opposed Diem. Rival factions in the South represented as much a danger to the government as the Vietcong. Diem had tended to favor his fellow Catholics. This caused great concern among the non-Christian groups. Prominent among these opponents were the Buddhists. When, on May 8, 1963, troops and police shot at Buddhist and student demonstrators in Hue, the unrest in the South reached new heights. Worldwide press coverage of a Buddhist monk setting fire to himself in Saigon in June in protest against the treatment of Buddhists left a great deal of unease. Diem's response did nothing to overcome this emergency. After August 21, when his forces attacked Buddhist temples, the demonstrations and self-immolations increased.

Diem overthrown and executed

Dissatisfaction among his army commanders was also being discussed. There had been various unsuccessful attempts to overthrow Diem. By the summer of 1963, Saigon was rife with rumors of coups being plotted. However, there were several factions among the army and air force vying for power, and each was uncertain of American reactions to a confrontation with Diem. When, in October, the Americans signaled that they would not interfere in any coup, a coalition of officers opposed to Diem was finally organized. On November 1, the Diem regime was overthrown and replaced by a government headed by General Duong Van Minh. Diem was shot the following day.

General Duong Van Minh (front row, sixth from the left) led the coup which overthrew Diem. Here he is with the leading members of his government.

This young Buddhist priest burned himself to death in Saigon in 1963 in protest against religious discrmination.

In deciding not to intervene, the United States had effectively sanctioned the toppling of Diem. The US had become increasingly irritated with his ineffectiveness in fighting the Vietcong and hoped that a new government would be more successful. However, the military infighting for positions of power continued. Diem was replaced by a series of inept and corrupt military leaders. Rather than stopping, the rot had only just begun. To fight the war effectively, it became increasingly clear to the Americans that they would have to commit their own combat troops. The *Maddox* incident and the turmoil in the South provided the justification and reason for that commitment.

6
Into the mire

Ten years after the Geneva Accord and the outbreak of civil war, the Vietcong controlled forty percent of South Vietnam. As American support for the South increased, so did the North's for the Vietcong. Each side was becoming increasingly committed to a military victory; neither could back down. Having established the importance of Vietnam to its policy of containment, the United States was unable to back away from the escalating conflict. With the failure of the South Vietnamese government to gain any major advantage over the Vietcong, the US was slowly pulled into the military conflict.

President Johnson with ministers of the Vietnamese government in Washington in 1966.

However, the more support she gave, the less credible became the idea of an independent South Vietnam. With the arrival of American troops, the Vietnamese were reminded of their colonial past. Throughout the period of American military intervention, demonstrations against the United States in the South took place, the Buddhists, once again, taking a leading role. These demonstrations were often reported as being Communist inspired, but there is little evidence for this. For the Vietnamese, they were once again fighting against foreign intervention in their country. In this situation, it was the Vietcong who gained. Untarnished by any previous cooperation with colonial forces and drawing upon their Vietminh past, they were able to draw a convincing picture of themselves as the true nationalists. American military intervention, therefore, did not stop the turmoil, but only added to it.

The problem for the American government was to justify

This village is a resettlement region into which people were moved from areas controlled by the Vietcong.

Opposite *One of the Vietcong's lethal booby traps: the spiked wooden frame would fall on an unsuspecting victim who had broken a trip wire.*

military involvement to the American people. President Johnson, who came to power after the assassination of John F. Kennedy in November 1963, held back for many months from his military commanders' request for direct intervention. The *Maddox* incident increased the pressure on him. However, it was only after a series of Vietcong raids against American installations in South Vietnam that President Johnson authorized the sustained bombing of the North, on February 24, 1965, and the commitment of troops in March. To the American public, this intervention was portrayed through the media as a response to Communist aggression from the North. However, evidence suggests that there were very few North Vietnamese in the South at this time and that it was only *after* the arrival of American troops that the North began to send its own troops to the South. It must also be remembered that the North considered itself Vietnamese, and so its involvement in the South was seen not as foreign aggression, but as the defense of one nation. However, the management of public opinion in the US was as important as the military effort in Vietnam. Optimistic forecasts of a swift end to the war were repeated in most media reports.

Mounting casualties
A swift victory was unlikely. The Americans were fighting in an unknown country, using tactics designed for conventional warfare. The rural-based guerrillas knew they could not win conventional battles, as the defeat of North Vietnamese troops in the La Drang valley in October 1965 showed. The Vietcong relied on small-scale night-time raids, disappearing back into the forests when danger loomed. To combat them, the Americans pursued a policy of search and destroy. Troops would move into an area controlled by the Vietcong to eradicate their influence. However, they found it impossible to distinguish ordinary peasants from Vietcong fighters. The indiscriminate killing of civilians continued and, when the Americans had moved on, the Vietcong could quickly reestablish control. Free-fire zones were created. Villagers were moved from areas controlled by the Vietcong. The American and South Vietnamese armies would then bombard the area and call in large-scale air strikes. The Vietcong ambushed patrols and booby-trapped forest pathways, making each step the American troops took a dangerous one. On all sides the casualties mounted.

Opposite *In Vietnam, first-class equipment and training were of little use to American troops against an invisible enemy.*

34

American soldiers land in an area that has been subjected to four days of heavy artillery fire and several bombing raids.

In this situation, a diplomatic solution to the conflict became impossible. Negotiations were fruitless, as the United States demanded the withdrawal of North Vietnamese troops and the North demanded the withdrawal of American troops. Neither side was prepared to accept the demands of the other throughout the mid-sixties. In its desire to defend the "free world" from communism, the United States became more and more deeply embroiled in Vietnam. The fact that she was supporting a brutal and corrupt regime with little popular support caused the occasional nagging doubt, but she had no alternative. To have done otherwise would have been to admit that the policy of containment may have been misconceived. If an American president had been prepared to admit this, he would have been attacked for being an "appeaser." On becoming president in 1960, Kennedy had said that the United States would "pay any price" to defend freedom. By 1968, it was doing precisely this – and the price was very high.

7
The Tet Offensive

By the end of 1967, there were 500,000 American troops in Vietnam. For two and a half years there had been a ground and air offensive against the Vietcong and the North. Yet the supplies of aid and men to the Vietcong continued unabated and large areas of the South remained under their control. In the beginning, American troops had some impact on the course of the war, but as they discovered their inability to defeat the Vietcong, their own morale began to sag.

Some of the 500,000 American soldiers who were in Vietnam at the end of 1967.

Success against the Vietcong was measured purely by the "body-count" – the number of enemy killed. American military personnel and politicians continually claimed that the Vietcong's morale and support would be broken by the war. The military wanted an ever-increasing commitment to the war. They believed in the effectiveness of their own firepower. President Johnson held back from the military's full demands. He was worried about being seen to undermine the independence of the South Vietnamese government.

The belief in the effectiveness of firepower to break the Vietcong was largely misplaced. If anything, the slaughter inflicted by the use of napalm, defoliants, and cluster bombs probably increased support for the Vietcong among the rural population. In the North, American bombing of strategic installations had very little impact on the course of the war. There were few major installations to hit. Bridges would be bombed and rebuilt continuously. While the

Use was made of defoliants, like Agent Orange shown here, by American forces.

Opposite *Shells being primed for use in action against the Vietcong in 1968.*

bombing was seen by the Americans as an incentive to the North Vietnamese to seek peace, it was used by the North to encourage support for the war in the South. The bombing served only to increase the North Vietnamese's hostility to the Americans and they continued to make elaborate preparations to ensure that supplies continued to the South. (They were assisted by the fact that they were not generally producing their own war goods, but distributing the aid sent by the USSR and China.) Throughout 1966 and 1967, there were various diplomatic moves to promote a peace agreement, but each side was escalating the military conflict to strengthen its own negotiating position.

American Embassy attacked

It was against this background that a decisive point in the war occurred. On January 31, 1968, the Vietcong and North Vietnamese launched the Tet Offensive against the major cities and towns of the South. There had been increasing opposition to the Americans among the Southern population. The Communist leadership, therefore, hoped that a major offensive would spark off urban uprisings and drive a wedge between the Americans and the South Vietnamese. However, this proved misconceived. Opposition to the American and the South Vietnamese government among the urban population did not necessarily mean that they would support the Vietcong. Consequently, neither the Vietcong nor the South Vietnamese government received the support they had expected. In most of the South, the Offensive was little more than a gesture, although one expensive in human lives. However, it was an important gesture. The ability of the Vietcong to mount a raid on their embassy in Saigon shocked the Americans.

Nor was the Tet Offensive without military successes, most notably in the city of Hue. It was only after twenty-six days of fighting, on February 25, 1968, that American and South Vietnamese troops managed to regain control of the city from the Vietcong. On returning, they found that the Vietcong had carried out a reign of terror against suspected government sympathizers, killing several thousand and burying them in mass graves. With the shock of the ability of Vietcong to mount such an offensive came the horror at what they were capable of.

The Tet Offensive was in many ways a failure for the Vietcong. Militarily, the Vietcong were defeated with huge

Opposite *A devastated street in Hue, South Vietnam, which American and South Vietnamese forces recaptured after twenty-six days of fighting.*

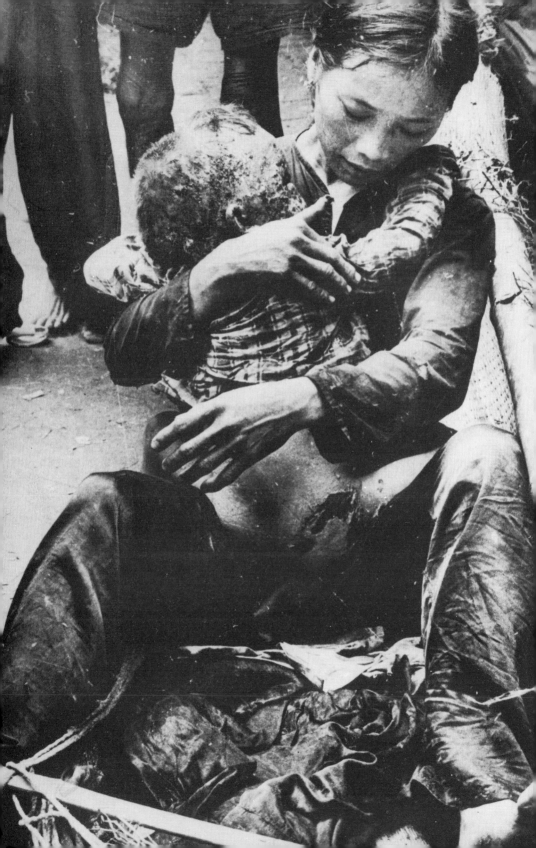

loss of life. The decimation of the Vietcong resulted in more Northerners being sent to the South to bolster the war effort. Increasingly, North Vietnamese personnel took over the leadership of the Vietcong. The Offensive's failure also had a bad effect on morale. Many considered it a mistake and a good deal of time was spent in regrouping after the South Vietnamese government had reestablished control of the cities. However, more important were the political and psychological effects that the Offensive had back in the United States, where there had been increasing opposition to American involvement in the war.

Two Vietcong soldiers lie dead after the unsuccessful attempt to capture the American Embassy in Saigon in January 1968.

Opposite *A mother tenderly holds her baby after it had been burned by nepalm.*

43

8
The antiwar movement

Opposition to the war in Vietnam among the American public began long before the Tet Offensive. Initially, it came from students hostile to being drafted into the armed forces. However, from 1966, as the casualty figures started to mount, wider opposition began to gain momentum. Church leaders and civil rights campaigners started openly to question the wisdom of the government's policy toward Vietnam. Senior politicians, including members of President Johnson's policymaking bodies, came to see military intervention as a mistake. The Tet Offensive further undermined confidence that the war could be won and accelerated the demands for an American withdrawal. Secretary of state for defense, Robert McNamara, who had supported the war in both the Kennedy and Johnson administrations, began to have severe doubts. He became a strong opponent of the war and was replaced in March 1968. Many former supporters went through similar changes of mind. Until he decided not to stand for reelection as president in 1968, Johnson was faced by two opponents of the war for the nomination as Democratic candidate, Eugene McCarthy and Robert Kennedy.

A media war
The American people were continually told by their leaders that the war was being won. It was the fact that no end to it came into sight that led many onto the streets to demonstrate against the continued involvement of the US in the war. The rising casualty figures, higher taxes to pay for the war, and inflation generated by that spending, did nothing to gain support for a war in a country that the majority of Americans had never heard of before American troops landed there in 1965.

The military and political supporters of the war blamed the media for the increasing opposition. But the media

Opposite *An anti-war demonstration in San Francisco in the late sixties.*

defended itself by arguing that it was simply portraying events, for which it was then accused of being unpatriotic. Editorially, it lagged behind public opinion in its expression of opposition to the war, even though daily reports on the war appeared in the newspapers and on television. It is often said that Vietnam was the first televised war. It is certainly true that images of wounded American troops, Vietnamese napalm victims, and the shooting of Vietcong suspects did affect public morale. Revelations, such as the massacre of over one hundred women and children by American troops in the village of My Lai, reported in November 1969 (although having occurred eighteen months earlier), shocked public opinion. The belief among Americans that it was right to be fighting in Vietnam came into question.

A draft dodger (second from right) being forcibly removed from a church in New York where he had sought sanctuary.

leged Vietnam Massacre
ndemned by White House

'Abhorrent to the Conscience Of All the American People'

By Robert Siner

WASHINGTON, Nov. 26.—The White House today condemned the alleged massacre of Vietnamese civilians by American troops as Song My as "abhorrent to the conscience of all the American people."

On Capitol Hill, senators said they were horrified by color slides of the alleged massacre shown to them by Army Secretary Stanley R. Resor.

In the first official White House comment on the incident in which U.S. soldiers reportedly killed more than 100 men, women and children, presidential press secretary Ron Ziegler said that the action was "in direct violation of U.S. military policy."

Mr. Ziegler said he was conveying "the overall feeling of the administration, and therefore of the White House, of the administration, and therefore of the President."

Mr. Ziegler said President Nixon was informed of the allegations

The antiwar movement became increasingly significant in American policy toward Vietnam. However, the extent of this opposition should not be overestimated. Opinion polls showed that although the majority of Americans came to view the war as a mistake, they also felt that, having become involved, the US should now stay and win. In November 1969, in the face of mounting opposition, Richard Nixon, who had been elected president in the previous November, rested his argument for the continued bombing of North Vietnam on the support of the "silent majority."

The bodies of innocent women and children lie on the road outside the village of My Lai. The massacre outraged the American nation.

47

However, it was the vocal minority that actively sought to change American policy. When, in 1970, four student antiwar protesters were shot dead by police, while demonstrating against the American invasion of Cambodia to destroy Vietcong bases, the shock waves were felt around the world.

Opposition to the war was not confined to the United States. Throughout the world during the late sixties and early seventies, huge demonstrations took place against American involvement, particularly in Europe. The US had

A TV news team film a gun-crew in action.

Opposite *One of the four protestors shot dead at Kent State University in 1970.*

49

argued that it had to fight communism in Vietnam to help keep the confidence of its Western Allies: If it could fight for a small country like Vietnam, it would certainly fight for Europe. However, most European governments thought the war a foolish venture that served neither Western nor American interests. Instead of enhancing the international reputation of the United States, the war, if anything, undermined it.

The end in sight

Thus, the war of attrition to wear out the Vietcong wore out American troops and public support for the war. As the American government's management of the news broke down and the reality of the war started to be presented to the public, vocal opposition to it certainly grew. To what extent this opposition forced the American government to search for ways out of the war is open to conjecture.

President Nixon justifying the decision to invade Cambodia in a televised speech.

9
Nixon's war

The diplomatic attempts to gain some form of peace settlement had been continually undermined by the military escalation of the conflict. However, the growing feeling among the Americans that they could not win the war led to the start of talks between the United States and North Vietnam in mid-May 1968. The Americans could not accept that they could be defeated and the military stalemate had to be broken. President Johnson had decided not to stand for reelection in order to promote the peace efforts. It was these

On June 8, 1969, President Nixon met President Thieu to tell him that the US planned to withdraw 25,000 troops that summer.

*Members of the
North Vietnamese
delegation at the
Paris peace talks in
May 1968.*

Opposite *July 1969:
The first of the
25,000 troops arrive
back on American
soil.*

efforts which Nixon inherited on becoming President. Nixon had always been a strong proponent of the war and was vehemently anti-Communist. However, the climate of opinion was changing and with it came the notion that the American aim should now be peace with honor. In January 1969 the peace talks in Paris were expanded to include the Vietcong and South Vietnamese government.

The Americans proposed a ceasefire and the withdrawal of American and North Vietnamese troops. This was unacceptable to the North Vietnamese, who saw the Americans as foreign interlopers, unlike themselves. Nixon's policy was to continue to put military pressure on the North to accept these terms. So he supported the increased bombing of the

North and, for the first time, the secret bombing of Vietcong bases in Cambodia. Linked with this was what was termed the "Vietnamization" of the war. American troops were to begin their withdrawal from Vietnam in June 1969, while military aid and assistance was increased to the South Vietnamese Army. The idea was that the latter, which in the early sixties was seen as incapable of the task, would now be able to keep the Vietcong at bay. The South Vietnamese Army was eventually to become one million strong, equipped with the latest American military technology. However, it continued to show its inability to combat the Vietcong, as in 1971, when it invaded Laos and unsuccessfully attempted to cut the supply of aid along the Ho Chi Minh Trail. The hope that the Vietnamization of the war would be militarily successful proved unfounded. However, American troop withdrawals continued. By the end of 1971, there were only 140,000 American troops in Vietnam.

Nor were Nixon's attempts to influence the peace talks confined to Vietnam. In February 1972, he met Mao Zedong in China and then, in May, President Brezhnev in Moscow. This was the beginning of the period of *détente*. In the sixties there had been increasing tension between the USSR and China, as they vied to extend their influence. Both Communist leaders were, therefore, looking to improve relations with the United States after the Cold War and also to gain support in isolating the other. Ho Chi Minh had gained support from both China and the USSR. On his death, on September 3, 1969, different factions within the Vietnamese Communist Party sought to move closer either to China or to the USSR to increase their support. In this, all factions were disappointed. After Nixon's talks, the USSR and China cut back their aid to the North, in order to pressurize it into seeking a treaty with the Americans.

Disillusioned American troops

Peace talks continued throughout 1972. In South Vietnam the conflict continued. However, the withdrawal of American troops was having adverse effects on the stability of the country. Many South Vietnamese government supporters considered the withdrawal a sellout to the Communists. Anti-American feeling was now widespread in the country. The American troops themselves became increasingly disillusioned. With the knowledge they were soon to go home, there was no incentive to risk their lives fighting

President Nixon meeting the Soviet leader, Leonid Brezhnev, in June 1974.

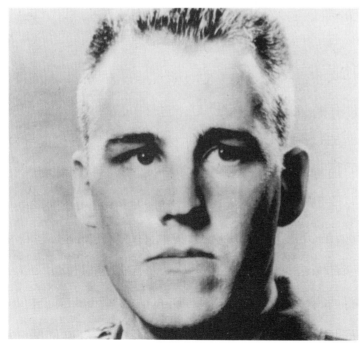

In August 1969, Lieut. Eugene Shurtz was relieved of command after his battle-weary troops rebelled against going into combat.

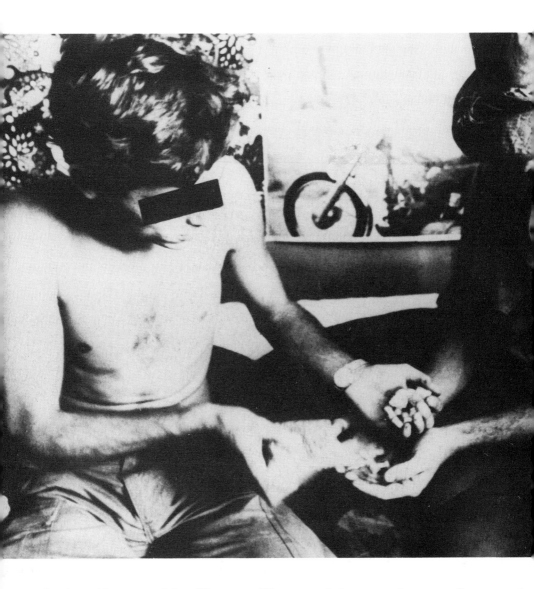

American soldiers taking drugs in Saigon.

the Vietcong. The use of drugs, such as marijuana and opium, became widespread. Insubordination increased. Officers who attempted to enforce discipline were often killed by their own troops. As the war drew to a close, South Vietnam was convulsed by uncertainty, which the mining of Haiphong and increased bombing did little to overcome. The Vietminh and Vietcong had fought for thirty-one years for a unified Vietnam and against foreign intervention. Time was on their side.

10
Peace, war, reunification

FOR THE GOVERNMENT OF THE
UNITED STATES OF AMERICA:

William P. Rogers
Secretary of State

FOR THE GOVERNMENT OF THE
DEMOCRATIC REPUBLIC OF
VIET-NAM:

Nguyen Duy Trinh
Minister for Foreign Affairs

The ceasefire agreement between the United States and North Vietnam was finally initialed in Paris on January 23, 1973, by Henry Kissinger and Le Duc Tho, and formally signed on January 27. However, the South Vietnamese government, under President Thieu, was implacably opposed to this agreement. When, in October 1972, the draft proposals had been presented to Thieu, he had put forward sixty-nine amendments. These had been objected to by the North

Signing the peace agreement in Paris on January 27, 1973.

57

A group of American prisoners of war being returned to American officials in Hanoi.

Vietnamese and, on December 18, Nixon had ordered the bombing of Hanoi and Haiphong. This was met with a storm of protest around the world and, after eleven days, the bombing was stopped. It is questionable whether this bombing was simply a symbolic gesture to reassure Thieu of continued American commitment to his government. But

Opposite *A street in Haiphong after twelve days of American bombing.*

the final ceasefire agreement in no way met his own demands.

The ceasefire allowed troops to remain where they were during the final withdrawal of American troops. A political settlement to the geographical and political partition of Vietnam was to be sought at a later date. While this left some areas of the South under Vietcong control, the military offensives of the previous year meant that Thieu controlled eighty percent of the country. On March 29, 1973, the last American troops left Vietnam and on April 1, American prisoners of war were released in Hanoi. Militarily, the American participation in the war in Vietnam had ended. The question was: what was going to happen next?

What did take place was the breakdown of the ceasefire. In January 1974, Thieu announced that the war had begun again. Whether or not in response to Vietcong violations of the ceasefire, the South Vietnamese Army began a major offensive against Vietcong-controlled areas. It is suggested that, fearful of his own position, Thieu redeclared war in order to force the Americans into committing troops to Vietnam, once again. However, the United States was weary of the war. Thieu did receive further military aid, but that was as far as the United States was willing to commit itself. It was itself in internal political turmoil over the revelations of the Watergate scandal, which was to force Nixon to resign from office in August 1974. In the military conflict with what was now a predominantly North Vietnamese army, it was the South Vietnamese Army that was to be the loser, in spite of American military aid.

South Vietnam surrenders

Beginning in June 1974, the Communists commenced a build-up of supplies and men in the South and, at the start of 1975, began a series of offensives against government-held areas. Unlike the Tet Offensive, which had mainly relied on Vietcong guerrillas, these attacks were dominated by North Vietnamese regulars under the overall control of General Van Tien Dung. The South Vietnamese Army collapsed in the face of this opposition. On March 25, the city of Hue, which Thieu had ordered to be defended at all costs, fell to the Communists. Then followed Da Nang on March 30, and on April 24 Xuan Loc, the last defense line before Saigon. The war was almost won. On April 25, Thieu left Saigon for exile in Taiwan, with the last American

Opposite *In January 1974, President Thieu of South Vietnam announced that the war had started again.*

61

Communist forces entering Saigon in April 1975.

officials being airlifted to waiting ships five days later.

On April 30, 1975, the Communists captured Saigon, with barely a shot fired. Colonel Bui Tin of the North Vietnamese Army accepted the surrender of the South Vietnamese government. The war was over. Vietnam had been reunified and was under Communist control. What the United States had fought against had happened, but she was in no mood to affect the final victory of the Communist-led nationalists.

11
America, post-Vietnam

On April 23, 1975, President Ford officially called the Vietnam War "finished." In the United States, there was generally relief that her involvement had come to an end. Officially and among public opinion, there was a general revulsion against discussing the war and an attempt to put it behind them. American troops returned from the war and found the heros' welcome they were expecting was not forthcoming. The American people, exposed to the media reports of massacres and drug abuse, did not feel proud of what their troops had been part of. Nor did many of the troops. Disabled veterans found themselves put into homes and hospitals and forgotten.

Vietnam veterans in a New York hospital where they are being treated for drug dependency.

LUIS E MUNIZ-GARCIA · HARRY T PETERSEN
WALDEMAR S GRZESKOWIAK
CURTIS RICHARD · RONALD E GARLAND
CHARLES G HUGHES · DANIEL J JEDNEAK
ROYCE L ADDINGTON · JOSE G BARRERA
FREDDIE L DACUS · TITUS L EPPS
JESSE L KESTLER · JOE BILLY McNETT
CRAIG T RESKA · WILLIAM L AIKEN
JOHN J FARNSWORTH Jr · ROBERT H GUMM Jr
ALVIN J SCOTT · JOHN G STRACHOTA
LEONARD P ALLEN · PAUL T COE
ROBERT SILAS ROCHA · FRANK R HITESHUE
JAMES M MEEHAN · PERRY A MITCHELL
CLARENCE R PRITCHARD Jr
VINCENT L ROSSI Sr · RICHARD W SALMOND
ROBERT G DRAPP · BRUCE L HANKINS
DEXTER J LOMBAS · JAMES F RILEY · JOHN M ROE
KENNETH D ADKINS
RUSSELL G DANIELS
ROBERT A DONNELL II
RANDALL P MANE
THOMAS L OSTEEN
WILLIAM E FLE
VERNON G Z
JAMES E ESKRIDGE
WARREN H MORLEY
TERRY F MEZERA
LEE D STUART Jr
WILLIAM B BLACKMON Jr
PERRY M SMITH
JOSHUA M DANIE
GLENN R ETHINGTON
ARTHUR S NABBEN
GREGORY S KARGER
RONNIE G VAU
HUGH D OPPERMAN
DONALD L SEN
RONALD J REVI
RICHARD C PORTER
JAMES P MARKEY Jr
KEITH
LUTHER N B
ROBERT L S
D COLEMAN
RICHARD W

The US was also facing its own domestic difficulties. The Watergate scandal had broken the trust which the public had traditionally put in its presidents. Also, the cost of the war was increasingly affecting the American economy. Government borrowing to pay for the war had generated higher rates of inflation. This was compounded by the oil crisis of 1973, when OPEC pushed up the price of oil, increasing the energy costs of the industralized nations.

However, despite the reluctance to discuss Vietnam, recriminations took place. The military blamed the politicians for putting constraints on the way they could handle the war. They accused the media and antiwar protesters of being unpatriotic and "appeasers" of communism. As the war became increasingly unpopular, politicians, worried about the chances of reelection, found the war an electoral liability. Spokespersons for the antiwar movement saw the whole war as a mistake, in which the United States had been embroiled as a result of misrepresentations of the true facts by the military and political leaders. What was largely missing in this debate and, to a certain extent, still is, is a realistic understanding of Vietnam as a nation.

Post-Vietnam lessons

The United States had been involved in a war in a country whose society and culture she did not understand. Decisions were taken in the expectation that the Vietnamese would respond in a similar manner to Americans. In this, they were disappointed. American policy continually failed, as with the Strategic Hamlets Program, because they did not foresee how the Vietnamese people would react. The Americans had largely made their own disaster in Vietnam.

In recent years, there has been a resurgence of the idea that the war could have been won, if only more military effort had been put into it. Whether this is, in fact, the case is open to question. It may have lengthened the war, but whether it could have been won and whether that victory would have been worthwhile can only be surmised.

The war does provide some lessons for American foreign policymakers. In Vietnam, they faced a Communist-led nationalist movement. To regard it merely as an instance of Communist aggression and expansionism was to simplify seriously and confuse the situation. Ho Chi Minh was a pragmatist and had wanted good relations with the US. When they were not forthcoming, the Vietminh was forced

Opposite A mother points out the name of her dead son on the Vietnam War Memorial which was opened in Washington, D.C. in 1982. The memorial has 57,939 names on it.

65

to become more reliant on the Communist bloc for support. Similarly, the American reliance on superior firepower to win the war, with material support for the brutal regimes of the South, led many nationalists into the Communist camp: the only body organized to fight for independence. Supporting dictatorships in defense of some notion of the "free world" produced hostility among the Vietnamese and did little to maintain the confidence of America's Western Alliance partners. The simplistic notions of Cold War confrontation underpinned American policy toward Vietnam, and, in many ways, undermined its ability to analyze realistically the emergence of Vietnam from colonial rule to national independence.

Flag-draped coffins of American servicemen killed in South Vietnam are placed in a plane for return to the US.

Whether such lessons have been learned by the foreign policymakers is open to question. However, a 1982 opinion poll, showing seventy-two percent of the American public against military invervention in Central America, suggests a greater reluctance to go to war now than existed at the time of the Vietnam War.

American prisoners of war land in Manila en route to their homes.

12
Vietnam: the aftermath

The war left Vietnam an economically, socially, and environmentally devastated country. The cost of reunifying the country had been immense. The Vietnamese politicians were faced with rebuilding their resource-rich country almost from scratch. This is something which is still far from complete. Vietnam remains one of the poorest countries in the world, suffering from famine, starvation, bureaucratic corruption, and inefficiency. This has been partly due to a lack of aid and partly due to mismanagement by the postwar government.

The inhabitants of Saigon watch the arrival of truck-loads of Communist soldiers in their city.

Goods intended only for sale at American bases on show on black market stalls in Saigon.

Guarded by a police boat, 160 Vietnamese "boat people" wait on a barge in Hong Kong harbor for immigration officials.

Large problems have resulted from the sheer loss of human life during the war. The death of large numbers of Vietcong meant that it was the North Vietnamese who took the major roles in organizing reconstruction. Regional difficulties between the North and South have asserted themselves. Many Northerners, schooled for three decades in the spartan conditions of the Communist North, resented the relative affluence of the South. Under the Americans, Saigon (now renamed Ho Chi Minh City) had become a city of bars, brothels, and bartering. In the eyes of the Northerners, this represented Western decadence, and harsh measures were taken to stamp it out.

70

Reeducation centers were established in the South. In many cases, these proved little more than prisons into which supporters of the previous government were put. However, it was not only government supporters who were forced into these centers. Many non-Communist nationalists also spent periods in detention. These people, largely the educated professionals of the South, could have been of great assistance in the rebuilding of Vietnam. However, their skills were wasted and the experience of detention made them resentful of the new government.

Kampuchea invaded

This situation worsened in December 1978, when Vietnam invaded Cambodia (renamed Kampuchea in 1975). In 1975, the Chinese-supported forces of Pol Pot, the Khmer Rouge, had taken over the country. They then proceeded to eliminate all opposition. The Vietnamese, fearful of an attempt by the Khmer Rouge to take control of the Mekong delta and with increasingly bad relations with China, moved first. Having finished one war, they then became involved in another. This resulted in Vietnam taking a more openly pro-Soviet stance, with the consequence that it became totally dependent on Soviet and East European aid.

The problem with that aid was that it was largely geared toward industrial development. In a rural society, this proved a disaster. Lacking the skills and spare parts to use them, large amounts of machinery have been left to rust. Meanwhile the agricultural areas have remained largely unaided. With the war in Kampuchea sapping manpower, food shortages have been common. Disillusionment with

The shattered remains of a South Vietnamese village destroyed during the war.

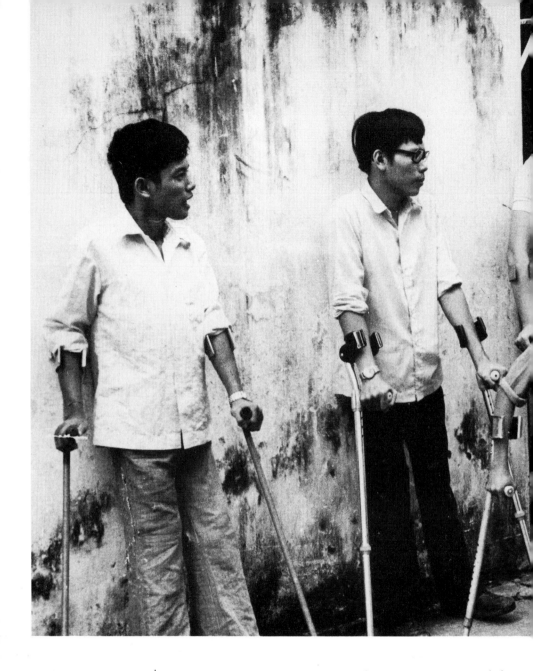

Vietnamese orphans of the war, crippled for life.

the Communist government and resentment toward its heavy-handed treatment finally resulted in the exodus of the "Boat People." Starting at the end of 1978 and still continuing, thousands of people have fled Vietnam in small boats across the South China Seas, a mark of the failure of the Communist government to handle the problems of

the country sympathetically.

In many ways, the tragedy of Vietnam continues. Cut off from large-scale aid, facing a war in Kampuchea, border battles with the Chinese, and an economy in ruins, the reunification of the country may have taken place, but the battle for its economic and social viability continues.

Glossary

Assassination   Planned murder, usually of a prominent public figure.

Attrition   Slow wearing away of an army's strength by incessant conflict on both sides.

Axis Powers   The alliance of Japan, Fascist Italy and Nazi Germany during World War II.

Body-count   The number of Vietcong and Vietnamese villagers killed during the War.

Cadres   Nonregular soldiers.

Capitulation   Military surrender.

Cartel   An association of independent companies formed to monopolize production of a commodity.

Cluster bombs   Bombs that scatter shrapnel over a wide area, causing widespread casualties.

Cold War   The state of political and military hostility between two powers, falling short of actual combat. The term usually applied to the situation between the United States and the USSR in the 1950s and 1960s.

Colonialism   The exploitation of one country by another for its resources.

Confucianism   The beliefs of Confucius, a Chinese philosopher, who lived from 551 to 479 B.C.

Containment   The policy of the United States toward communism in the post-World War II era.

Coup   A sudden takeover of a government by rebels.

Covert   Concealed or secret.

Defoliants   Chemicals sprayed onto the Vietnamese forest to remove cover essential for the Vietcong forces.

Democrats   One of the two political parties in the United States. The other is the Republicans.

Déntente   The short-lived agreement between the USA and the USSR to try to reach a position of peaceful coexistence; a relaxation of their hostilities.

Domino Theory   The idea that if Vietnam fell to the Communists, so would the whole of Southeast Asia, country by country (as dominoes knock each other over when placed upright in a row and one is tipped).

Free World   An American term for virtually all the non-Communist governments taken together.

Geneva Accord   Treaty signed on July 20, 1954, after the Vietminh victory at Dien Bien Phu, which ended the French wars in Indo-China.

Guerrilla   A member of an irregular army fighting the organized, regular forces of the state.

Indo-China   Vietnam, Laos, and Kampuchea (Cambodia).

Jesuits   The members of the Roman Catholic monastic order founded in 1534.

Khmer Rouge   The Chinese-backed Communists of Kampuchea.

Napalm   A form of jellied gasoline that sticks and sets fire to anything it touches.

Pacification   The program of aid for the South Vietnamese peasants, intended to remove them for Vietcong influence.

Self-determination   The idea that a people has the right to determine the way their country is run.

Self-immolation   Setting fire to oneself; a form of suicide that was performed by many Buddhist monks and nuns in Vietnam.

Tet   The lunar new year.

Totalitarianism   Nondemocratic, one-party rule.

Tribute   A payment to a stronger country by a weaker one, as a token of submission.

Unilateral   (In politics). When something involves or is done by only one party or country out of several, often without consultation.

Vietcong   Southern Communists, leading members of the opposition to South Vietnamese governments and the Americans.

Vietminh   Communist-led nationalist guerrillas who fought against the Japanese and French.

Vietnamization   The policy of returning the war effort to the South Vietnamese Army after the United States' decision to withdraw.

Watergate scandal   During the 1972 American presidential campaign, the Democratic headquarters (the Watergate Building) was broken into and burgled by agents of the Republican Party. As a consequence, president Nixon was forced to resign in 1974.

Index

Antiwar movement 43, 55–50,
  65

Bao Dai, Emperor 20, 22
Brezhnev, President 54
Britain 20

Cambodia (Kampuchea) 14, 25,
  54, 71, 73
China 12, 18, 19, 24, 41, 54, 71,
  73
Cold War 19, 54, 66

Da Nang 10, 61
Diem, Ngo Dinh 22, 25, 26, 27,
  28, 29, 30
Dien Bien Phu, Battle of 20
"Domino Theory" 19
Dung, Van Tien 61

Ford, President 63
France 12, 14, 15, 16, 19, 20, 21,
  50; see also Indo-China

Geneva Accord (1954) 21, 22.
  31
Gulf of Tonkin 8

Haiphong 16, 56, 59
Hanoi 16, 56, 61
Ho Chi Minh 14, 15, 16, 19, 21,
  54, 65
Ho Chi Minh Trail 25–6, 54
Hue 41, 61

Indo-China 14, 20
Indo-China Communist Party 14,
  15

Japan 15, 16
Jesuits 14
Johnson, President 34, 39, 44,
  51

Kennedy, President 34, 36, 44
Kennedy, Robert 44
Khmer Rouge 70
Kissinger, Henry 57
Korean War 18, 20

Laos 14, 25, 54

Maddox, USS 8, 9, 34
Mao Zedong 18, 54
McCarthy, Eugene 44
McNamara, Robert 44
Media 34, 44–5, 50, 62, 63, 65
Mekong River 24, 71
Minh, Duong Van 29
My Lai massacre 46, 47

Nixon, Richard 47, 52, 54, 59,
  61
North Vietnam 8, 9, 10, 21, 22,
  24, 25, 26, 31, 34, 36, 41, 43, 51,
  52, 57, 61, 62, 70, 71
  bombing of 10, 34, 39, 41, 47,
    52–3, 56, 59
  government 24
  war casualties 10–11

Paris Peace Accord (1973) 10, 52,
  57
Pol Pot 71

Religion 14, 22, 28–9, 33

Saigon 27, 29, 41, 61, 70
South Vietnam 8, 21, 30, 33, 34,
  39, 41, 43, 46, 54, 61, 62
  army 10, 34, 54, 61
  government 10, 22, 24, 26, 27,
    28, 30, 31, 43, 52, 57
  independence 22
  war casualties 11, 34, 46, 70
Strategic Hamlets Program 27–8,
  65

Tet Offensive 41–2, 44, 61
Thieu, President 57, 61
Tho, Le Duc 57
Tin, General Bui 62
Tu Doc, Emperor 14
Turner Joy, USS 8, 9

United States 15, 16, 17, 19, 20,
    22, 24, 26, 27, 29, 30, 31, 34,
    41, 44–50, 51, 52, 54, 61, 63
"containment" policy 18, 19,
    31, 36, 48
cost of war 10
numbers killed 11
"pacification" policy 27

troops in Vietnam 10, 27, 33
troop withdrawals 37, 61
United Nations 24
USSR 17, 18, 19, 20, 24, 41, 54,
    71

Vietcong 10, 25, 26, 27, 28, 30, 31,
    33, 34, 37, 39, 41, 43, 46, 50,
    52, 54, 56, 61, 62
number killed 11
Vietminh 15, 16, 18, 19, 21, 22,
    24, 25, 33, 56, 65–6

Watergate scandal 61, 65
World War II 10, 14, 15, 16, 17,
    18, 19, 20

Picture acknowledgments

The publishers would like to thank the following for allowing their photographs to be reproduced in this book: Associated press *cover*, 39, 47 (main picture), 48, 63, 66; BBC Hulton Library *frontispiece*, 36, 37, 38; Camera Press Ltd 10–11, 19, 21, 25, 32, 35, 45, 49, 55 (top), 57 (both), 58, 59, 64, 68, 71, 72–3; Mary Evans Picture Library 12; Robert Hunt Library 17, 31, 50; Popperfoto 18, 40, 43, 56, 62, 67, 69, 70; TOPHAM 8, 9, 20, 23, 24, 28, 29, 30, 33, 42, 46, 47 (inset), 51, 52, 53, 55 (bottom), 60; Embassy of the Socialist Republic of Vietnam 15, 16. The maps of pages 13 and 26 were drawn by Malcolm S. Walker.